MEDIUM SPEED IN THE CITY CALLED PARIS

POEMS, VOL. 1

AMIR SAID

Superchamp Books SB

Medium Speed in the City Called Paris:
Poems, Vol. 1
By Amir Said

Copyright © 2016 by Amir Said.

A Superchamp Books First Paperback Edition

All rights reserved.
No part of this book may be reproduced in any form by any electronic or mechanical means, including information storage and retrieval systems, without the expressed written permission of the publisher, except by a reviewer, who may quote brief passages in a review. Published by Superchamp Books, Inc. P.O. Box 20274, Brooklyn, New York 11202-0274. www.superchampbooks.com; Twitter: @SuperchampBooks; @amirsaid; Facebook: Superchamp Books

Assistant Editor: Amir Ali Said

Photographs:
Cover photo by Maxcam Copyright © 2016 Maxcam
Back Cover photo of author by Amir Said © 2016 Amir Said

Cover, Design, and Layout by Amir Said

Print History:
August 2016: First printing.

Medium Speed in the City Called Paris: Poems, Vol. 1 / by Amir Said
1. Said, Amir 2. Poetry 3. Paris—Culture 4. New York City—Culture
5. Paris—Social Aspects 6. New York City—Social Aspects 7. Popular Culture—France 8. Popular Culture—United States I. Title

Library of Congress Control Number: 2016913628
ISBN 978-0-9893986-9-5

For my son, Amir Ali Said.
Amir, nobody can be a better you than you.
("When the door opens for opportunity,
walk through.")
Insha'Allah…Al-Humdullilah.

CONTENTS

INTRODUCTION	1
PART 1: THE CITIES	7
Stardust on a Gloomy Night	8
I Will Show You How to Eat in Paris	9
My Dear Deranged New York	10
Medium Speed in the City Called Paris	12
Dis-moi	13
Buzz	14
Spices	15
Tropes of the Same Americans in Paris	16
The Object of the Game at Bars in New York	17
The Object of the Game at Bars in Paris	18
Curvy in Paris	19
Coming Upon Love from Barbès Rochechouart	20
How Does Anybody Get Anything Done in Paris	21
The Girl with Turquoise Hair and Mirrored Shades	22
Je te connais	23
Near Rue de Duras	24
I Want to Be President	25
On Becoming Familiar with the Cadence of Parisians	26
Un Vélo dans la lumiére du soleil	27
Try	28
Pardon	29

Sugar on Pocorn	30
Wonderlight	31
Outside the Jamaican Food Spot on Nostrand, Just Off Fulton	32
The Duty of a Smoker Sitting Closest to the Street at a Café in Paris	33
My Neighbors in Paris Know Me and I Know Them	34
Do You Feel Free	35
Because I'm Running Late	36

PART 2: LOVE, AFFAIRS, AND BROKEN PEOPLE — 37

Why Are They All Amazed	38
I Will Jump In	39
You Would Rather	40
Polite Talk At a Dinner Party	41
For When Women Speak of Feminism on First Dates	42
Fools Like to Smell Red Roses in the Winter Time and Magicians Always Give Away Their Best Tricks	43
Not Long After I Had Left	44
When We First Kissed	45
It Was Only Supposed to Be Fun (or, When the Wall's Crumble Down On an Open Relationship Because the Whole Damn Thing Was Fraudulent From the Beginning)	46
Sex Sells	48
Always More Red Wine	50

We Were a Perfect Match	51
Lovers Will Promise Anything in Bed	52
Less Than Whole	54
Advice for Men and Women in the Online Dating Age	56
Fat & Greedy	58
She Doesn't Want to Marry You Anymore	60
Dodge	62
I Overheard an Ex-Girlfriend	63
Fuck, Make Love, and Do Shit Together	64
The Failure of Scorned Women and Men	65
A Mother Teaching Her Daughter How to Ride Bikes	66
Soon	68
The Good Panties	69
So Long As You Cherish	70
The Water Moves for the Swimmer	71
A Poem for Qamar	72
PART 3: EAST WIND WRITERS WORKSHOP	**73**
I Wanna Be Somebody, So Bad	74
Add Water	75
The Luxury of Not Thinking Anymore	76
How Do You Explain to a Little Black Girl Sitting in the Back Seat	78
Grabbing a Rocketship with One Hand and Drinking an RC Cola	80
The Darkies Are on Main Street	81
The Great American Novel, Some Pussy on the Side, and a Few Other Things	82

My Mother Left a Message on My Phone   84
Your Heroes Have Holes in Their Wings   86
Idiomatic Ways of Speech
(or, Two Old Friends from East New York, Brooklyn
Running Into Each Other by Chance)   87
Issues in the News: A Letter to Jack   88
Get Down to It   89
Pay Me   90
You Better Read   92
The Bleachers   93
Is It Because I'm Black
(Dedicated to Uncle Syl Johnson)   94
Black People Jump High   96
Generation Nothing   97
A Rhyme for Qamar
(That's Why Amir is So Wild)   99

PART 4: THE CLASSICS   101
A Poem for Spring   102
All the Fools Rush in the Rain   103
You Love Not Me   104
A Poem for Jamie Claar   105
All That Melts   106
Ask Me Where I've Been   107
A Poem for My Brooklyn Crew   108
So Clear of Victory   109
What Will They Know
(Poem #2 for My Son, Amir Ali Said)   110
Certainty is the Fool's Tambourine   112
The Fair Lady of Baskerville   113

A Poem for Sheila Fraizer	114
Simple Equations	115
A Poem for Marina Keegan	116
The Future of Goodbye	117
Knowledge is a Reward Most Giving	118
A Poem for Clara	119
My First Touch of Spring	120
Artificial Intelligence (A.I.)	122
A Poem for Uncle Prince	123
Looking at Picture Books with a 3-Year-Old Boy Who Already Reads and Watches Alfred Hitchcock Movies at Lunch (Poem #3 for My Son, Amir)	124
Hills of Grass	125
A Writer I Know Gave Herself a Man's Name	126
Let Me Tell You About My Son, Amir (Poem #4 for My Son, Amir)	127
Garbage Lady	128
The Arrogant Masters of Time	129
Love of Forsaken Town	130
If Today Was When We Met	131
The Rangers	132
A False Invention	133
Crest and Crown	134

PART 5: THE SPOILS OF HUMANITY — 135

The Dimming Glow of Youth (or, Posing Not Far From République)	136
Why Would Anyone Care About Me	137
The First Place We'll Eat Toger	138

Too Far Gone	140
She Could Not Wait (for K.E.)	142
Rumi Says Pay Attention to How Things Blend and Eddie Says He Knows It's a Rotten Game	144
A Bird Looking Back At You Curiously	145
Most Girls Grow Up to Be Brave Women	146
Be Leery of Their Disguise	147
When We Switched on Computers	148
Samuel Jackson Don't Say No to Movies	150
The More You Know, the More You Will Lose People	151
You Will Know Somebody	152
If You Allow Yourself to Be Invisible	154
Go Deeper	157

ACKNOWLEDGEMENTS   159

Introduction

"Cities, like people, can be recognized by their walk."
—Robert Musil

Having recently written *The Truth About New York*, a book that works as a cultural study that, among other things, spotlights the main components that drive the pace of New York City, I was in a space that left me deeply drained yet oddly reinvigorated. On the one hand, it's impossible to examine New York City and not come away exhausted. On the other hand, such a deep exploration inevitably renews your affection for one of the world's greatest, most thrilling and complex cities. But surprisingly (or perhaps not so for various reasons), my renewed love for New York could not displace what Paris has come to mean to me.

For the past four years I've come to Paris, learning this city's ways and actions a little more each time. And what I now know and love about this city the most is its pace. Paris is never as break-neck fast or hazardous as New York, but it's certainly not a slow town either. After all, it is a big city and one of the world's finest major international posts. But for all of its big-city bonafides, Paris has a pace that is quite curious, a pace that I like to call *medium speed*.

I am not a farmer who desires the stillness and simplicity of life on a farm. And I am certainly not a recluse who favors the uncapped tranquility of an isolated life in a cabin somewhere in the middle of the woods. But I share a farmer's appreciation for a simpler life; and the cabin recluse and I have a common link in our recognition of the benefits to being alone with one's thoughts. So this is the contradiction that I've come to embrace in my life. I'm staunchly, and necessarily, a city person. I need and thrive on the nature of city. Too much tranquility, too much stillness, too much isolation and not enough blended culture is not for me. But too much speed, too many available thrills, and an always-on, hustle-until-you-die pace (and mentality) doesn't quite fit me either; or at least it doesn't fit me anymore.

For me, Paris's medium-speed pace is more about *taking* life in and less about *fitting* life in. Paris is alive, and it has a big-city rush, but it also has an older, easier sense of pace. A mix of quaint with the modern pace of things. A pace well-suited for the kind of thinking and reflection I like to do. Actually, what it is that I do most in Paris is think and walk. And more than anything else, I'm grateful to this city for being a place just right for me to do that.

Naturally, the poems in this volume (all written in Paris in 2016), represent many of the thoughts and reflections that I had during my time spent in here. But while a number of poems in this volume of *Medium Speed...* are directly or indirectly related to Paris in some way, this collection of poems is certainly not only about Paris. Which is to say that this book is not restricted to the physical (and mental) borders of Paris (or New York). Rather, it contains an array poems that detail a palate of perceptions and understandings, classic observations of humanity and culture, and, of course, self-discovery and exploration. All of which I was able to see and process more clearly while here in Paris.

About the Slant of the Poems in this Volume

The poems in this volume of *Medium Speed...* reflect my varied experiences, perspectives, and contradicting — but not always conflicting — interests. While my voice is consistent throughout this collection, the tenor, timbre, feel, and touch varies. For instance, the base of my poetry style stems from the 1960s/1970s black American poetry or "rap" tradition. But there are a number of poems in this collection that are influenced by 19th century British and American poetry styles as well.

Stylistic descriptions notwithstanding, the poems presented in this volume bear the mark of who I am: A man who has been hardened by life, yet not too far gone to appreciate, celebrate, and remember those beautiful moments that I've enjoyed and experienced along my path. Thus, the poems in this volume not only reflect my world (or worlds) and sensibilities for everything from love to art to history to society, they also reflect my true voice, how I speak and communicate. In other words, there are some relatable truths (I hope) in this collection of poems; and as such, the language of some poems is direct and hard at times and perhaps more gentile at others. Likewise, while there's not a terrible amount of profanity in this collection, please be advised that some profanity does appear.

I would also like to note that, while I am consumed with design and fonts when it comes to overall book design, I do not carry the same enthusiasm for type when it comes to presenting poetry. I place no emphasis on using unique fonts, extra small or extra large font sizes, unusual line breaks or spacing, or any other visual effects. I firmly believe that words on the page should function as, well, words on the page: They should help readers to navigate an expression — as seamlessly as possible and without undue distraction — that an author wants to offer. If the words of a poet's poems "speak" on the page, then it is simply that poet's fortune that readers hear their voice.

Finally, I have organized the poems in this volume into five parts: **The Cities; Love, Affairs,** and **Broken People; the Classics; East Wind Writers Workshop,** and **the Spoils of Humanity.**

The Cities contains reflections of some of my experiences in various cities, most prominently Paris and New York, and highlights some of the thoughts culled from those places.

Love, Affairs, and Broken People is just that: A seranade to the challenges of finding love, the realities of affairs, and the inevitable joys and fallout of it all.

The Classics includes some of poems written in more traditional meter; and subjects in this part run the gambit. I've also designated this part as place for poems that I've written specifically for various people who have touched my life in one way or the other.

East Wind Writers Workshop borrows its name (and calling) from the 1968 East Harlem black writers workshop called *East Wind*. For me, East Wind symbolizes a poetic feel and philosophy, a guiding literary force that has informed and, in some ways, shaped all of my writings. Thus, East Wind has become the short-hand term that I use to describe the era of black American creativity that has had the most profound influence and effect on my creative psyche. This part of *Medium Speed...* features examples of what I like to call the *East Wind* rhythm of poetry; and I offer this part as homage to the black American poets of the *East Wind* era whose shoulders I stand on.

The Spoils of Humanity includes poems that spotlight specific nuances of the human experience: Our triumphs and our failures; our kindness and our evilness; our courage and our fears; the inevitability of pain and the ongoing pursuit of happiness. Life is a daily mix of joy, pain, certainty, uncertainty, surprise, shock, and the expected, confusion, and solution. And that's what I want this collection of poems to reflect.

Said (Amir Said),
Paris, France
29, July, 2016

The Cities

Stardust On a Gloomy Night

There is no stardust
on a gloomy night
above grand avenues.
If you hear laughter,
it is not a situational comedy
or a teenage prank
gone good and awry.
Through winding walkways
of Les Batingolles,
which is a window washing La Défense,
the echoes of aperitifs float
and bounce, and grant you well.
Otherwise in other places,
in other cities of noble regard,
this is a rhythm captured,
tucked too deep
and hidden away from me,
even on brighter nights.
But for a word, a full phrase,
a grasp of the talk,
I would have been able
to accept what was kindly being
offered as I walked.

I Will Show You How to Eat in Paris

I will show you how to eat in Paris.
Slowly, and with more frequent pause.
With the effort of a gold canary or a blue ox,
eat with your heart and taste with your ears.

I will show you how to eat in Paris.
In good company, and with an open league of discussion.
With cotton blues and denim news,
it is nay the cold rule of consumption.

I will show you how to eat in Paris.
Wisely, with a keen sense for the kitchen
and the sprouting delights of the season.
With a simple appetite and a nurtured palette.

I will show you how to eat in Paris.
Late, with an affection for the buzz of the quarter.
With a calm excitement and a happy reserve.

My Dear Deranged New York

My dear deranged New York,
looking back at you from Paris,
the madness makes more sense.
The bruises you dish out.
The non-stop, overflowing
buckets and slices of people.
The broad schism of noises
you hear in the bellies of fun,
tragedy, delight, and wonder.

The collision all makes sense.
You peel hope from your locals,
the main fee for drinking your air.
But you pay in spades of opportunity.
You are the drunk uncle driving home.
The young mugger smoking a bone.
The stylish fixer.
The sophisticated trickster.
All the wild white girls who left home.
You are the strides of new identity.
A dirty splint on a crushed leg.
You are too arrogant to wait for anyone,
but exact in your patience
for those who groove like Nutmeg.

You pick apart clowns
and shield frauds from light.
There's no box you can't think out of,
no cuisine you can't score
on a lazy Sunday night.
You have no lazy Sunday nights
because the show is always on with you.

You are always peeking over your shoulder,
slicing your shadow into 8 million vestibules.

You are a happy con artist
smiling at a nervous wreck.
A disco in a warehouse.
A garage orgy of free sex.
Your curtains close only
for the next dishwashing gig.
You beg no one to embrace you,
and this is all that it is:
My dear deranged New York,
let us remember the things we did.

Medium Speed in the City Called Paris

Don't tell me Paris moves fast.
This place moves at medium speed.
There are no stand stills
like in butter-slow Amsterdam.
And you won't find too many
peedy moments like in manic London,
or my dear deranged New York.
This is because Paris likes to watch.
And talk.
And talk.
Paris loves her voice,
and with every good reason to do so.
Her rhythms tumble and flow,
echo and glow.
And everyone's in on the secret.
Paris is nobody's in between.
But she sits in a seam
with a movement that's green
in all of her medium sequence.
Days never blur but blend.
Nights never cave but bend.
And there are no twilight hours
to ever discover beneath it.
Paris is medium speed.
A bridge with unpolished cobbled rocks
and motorcycle motors.
A prolonged glance at a movie poster,
and a canal near simmering aromas.
This is a town where *Bonjour*! moves a frown.
A city where action goes with no effort.

Dis-Moi

Tell me again about the smells
of La Chappelle.
The slickness and baggage
at Barbès Rochechouart.
Tell me about the sun-orange
and rays of golden light
bouncing on the canal.
Tell me about the patter
at Gare du Nord
and the North Brooklyn-like bars
in Oberkampf,
and the woman who wants you
to take salsa lessons
around the corner
from Parmentier.
Tell me again about the curry
and kebab of La Chappelle.
The bronze-colored women
with bread in their hips and ass,
the two lovers kissing in Stan Smiths,
the four mothers teaching
their children how to share a laugh.

Buzz

I like the buzz of construction
and the car horns in conjunction.
The rumbling quake of enterprise,
the exchange all in function.
The pulse, smoke, debris, and patter.
The ghost notes from wrecking balls,
the shovels, the scrapers, and all manner of hammers.
I am fundamentally, unequivocally,
pro rock-steady for the city.
I am not a farmer, I've seen some drama,
I approach blocks sensibly.

Spices

Food markets and fresh ingredients.
But don't go looking for any spices in Paris,
is what a fool told me.
Fresh bread and tasty pastries.
But this is not a place for spices,
is what a moron told me.
Cafés with steak as you might like.
Bars with wine and beer
will be the regular each night.
But forget about having any spices
in this city, is what an idiot told me.
Standing in the supermarché at Victor Hugo,
right in front of the spice rack,
I'm happy because they have restocked my favorite.

Tropes of the Same Americans in Paris

The megaphone noise
about the French —
and by proxy I mean Parisians —
is that they are rude,
and they always complain.
This is typically supported by fat Americans
on vacation who've had to wait too long
for their extra side of fries.
Or it's propped up by posing Francophiles,
hooked on chasing the ghost of Hemingway
inside their beloved Saint-Germain.
Or this story is told by narrow-ass New Yorkers,
up speaking at all-white parties,
about all-white things.
But this story is never told by those of us
who are not the same Americans;
those of us who have never had to deal
with the nagging problem of getting our way.
Those of us who have never been forced
to take advantage of all the hidden perks
and routine benefits showered upon us
everyday just because.
For us, Paris is no trope,
nor perfected city;
just a home that feels more home
than the lies told on T.V.

The Object of the Game at Bars in New York

Gather information.
Ask innocent questions
designed to gather information.
Ask direction questions that are really
designed to gather indirect information.
Ask them what do they do for a living.
Ask them if they have any brothers or sisters.
Ask them how often do they speak
to their mother or father, brother or sister.
Record the so-far information,
then do more intense probing.
Press them about their last relationship.
Press them about why their last relationship ended.
Press them about their living situation.
Press them again about their living situation.
Press them about how often they drink.
Press them about using drugs.
Press them about what they like to do
(and remember to act like you care).
Press them about the last time
they went out on date and what happened.
Press they about what they like to eat.
All the while, flirt, to see how far you can get;
drink, until you're not really drunk, but just drunk;
then invite yourself to their place
if they don't have any roommates at home.

The Object of the Game at Bars in Paris

Speak French.

Curvy in Paris

In Paris, Curvy is not
the euphemism for fat
that many white American women
make it be.
Curvy is a fact of femininity,
an action of sexuality.
Curvy is not brown bag lunch,
or an undesirable pick.
Curvy in Paris
is black American soul woman
proudly walking her hips.
Curvy is not fat lies
told on OKCupid.
Curvy in Paris
is an alluring silhouette
amazed by its own movement.
Curvy in Paris
is not a construct
for isolating chubby in one line.
Curvy in Paris
is all the fresh bread
and possibly all the red wine.

Coming Upon Love from Barbès-Rochechouart

I left Barbès one day,
heading east.
On Rue Polonceau,
I met a organizer
who was so kind to speak.
No more than a block
from where we stood,
I made a photograph
of a bridge I've seen
in every hood.
I passed by a woman
negotiating the fall
of two heavy boxes.
She smiled,
and they fell,
neither of us could stop it.

How Does Anybody Get Anything Done in Paris

I still haven't figured out how
anything gets done in Paris.
In New York, I see the hustle.
I see the people bent down,
knuckles dragging on the ground.
When a new building is made
in the Big Apple, I feel wiped out
right along with the workers.
In the city that never sleeps,
I know what it means to be
pummeled by the speed of things.
But here in Paris,
buildings are made by workers
who aren't busy beating
themselves into the ground.
And even when people do
move fast in Paris,
they move smooth;
never just plain ol' rat-race fast.
So I just don't understand how
anyone gets anything done
in this town. But surely they must.
I mean, the métro runs better.
The food is always fresh.
The wine never ends.
The philosophies keep going.
Enough movie theaters to start a village.
Everybody's always going on
or coming back from holiday.
So how are they doing all of this?

The Girl With Turquoise Hair and Mirrored Shades

They dragged you to Paris.
You didn't want to come here.
Because you don't like nowhere.
You don't like anything.
And everybody gets on your nerves.
And don't nobody understand you but Weezer.
You had to come to Paris
because you can't be trusted at home alone.
You might kill yourself.
And literally nobody cares,
so why do they want you around
in the first place?
What are you supposed to get
from Saint-Germain and Pigalle,
the Eiffel Tower and Champs Élysées?
You can stick to yourself back home.
You can be all alone and roam
inside your miserable life
back in that slow hometown
you didn't ask to be from.
You didn't want to come Paris,
but you needed to come to Paris
because your old man likes family vacations
and he wants you and your princess sister
to get along like you used to.

Je te connais

I helped an elderly woman
find her way in the 16th.
She stopped me to ask for directions.
In front of her, just before I arrived,
there were no less than ten people
she could have asked.
All of which certainly spoke
better French than me.
But she reached out and grabbed my arm,
"Excusez-moi, Monsieur."

Near Rue de Duras

Two armed police officers, a police van,
and some damn good day light,
and this white lady from America clutched,
then jerked, her purse as she walked towards me.
Eight armed guards clearly stamped
in military green and brown fatigues,
wearing machine guns,
a lazy open-air day with damn good sunlight,
and this high-nose white lady clutches her bag
as she walks towards me.
I'm standing near Rue de Duras on a damn fine day,
dressed in my everyday way
(so you know I'm sharp, clean, and mean)
and on three sides of me, it's police, soldiers,
and mad gallery goers,
and this white bitch from America
clutches her bag as she walks towards me.

I Want To Be President

"I want to be President,"
the little girl from Indonesia said to me.
Inside the Sunday morning rush of a bubbling
Rotterdam Central Tickets and Service office,
she told me she wanted to be President.
She used no article in front of "President".
A wise choice; kids see things as plain as they are.
She was traveling with her family.
Her cousins, a girl just shy of four
and a boy still peaking at two,
shadowed her every word and move.
Sitting beside me on my right, her uncle,
kind, pleasant, and visibly a good father,
spoke of tobacco and its demand in Indonesia.
On my left was her grandfather.
Still enamored by the photos on his iPad
that he'd just taken of the family,
he called out with his hands
for his grandson to come to him.
Grandson having arrived,
Grandfather told him
to "Say hello" to me.
Uncle (and Father) then asked me
what I do for a living.
I told him I was a writer and publisher.
"Publishing?!" Grandfather interjected,
his plus-50 years now vibrant and electric.
"I am a publisher, well, I used to be," he said.
"I started in 1979.
Now my daughters run the company."

On Becoming Familiar with the Cadence of Parisians

On becoming more familiar
with the cadence of Parisians.
The process is not sordid,
nor as awkward as outsiders
do often suggest.
The exchange is even,
all at once a fittingly odd blend
of rhythm in blue minor.
Once you see the timbre
and hear the marks of this city's style,
you are brought further in,
near where the river bends,
and where the canal soothes your brow.

Un vélo dans la lumiére du soleil

In a cup of coffee,
in a small café near
Strasbourg Saint-Denis,
you can see the despair.
It glistens as a mirror,
showing the macabre
that has gathered
along the huddled sidewalk.
The garbage collectors
have crushed the bike
of a woman who had locked it
to a small pole.
And in the maze of complaint,
grief, and strange cheer,
the broken bike is now
beautiful art in the sunlight.

Try

Try not chasing every thrill
New York shoves your way.
I wanna see you try not blowing
a whole night away because
you can't decide on a place
to eat. Because it's too many
damn places to eat.
Too many damn places to sleep
with broken people and dreamers
walking barefoot through tunnels.
Just try to hold back the urge
to fall into four things in one night.
A party somewhere in (the new) Bed Stuy.
Another party up on the Upper West Side.
A gallery in Chelsea.
A sex club on the Bowery.
An impromptu meeting with a girl
named Yessenia and her best friend Mallory.
I wanna see you say no to that.
I wanna see you try to not soak up
all the arts New York throws your way.
Graff writers. Guggenheim.
Webster Hall. Brooklyn Bowl.
The Bell House. MoMA. The Met.
The Whitney. Five hundred damn Broadway Shows.
BAM. And there's even a museum of Sex.
Try not doing all of that.
Just go ahead and try not finding your way.
Try not seeing what it feels like to be in New York,
Chillin' on Eastern Parkway taking
in the West Indian Day Parade.

Pardon

Outside on the corner by La L'Orraine,
a boy twirled in his innocence
while his mother spoke
on the phone with a friend.
With each spin,
you saw the dizziness grab hold
a little more, until he crashed
into my leg and said, "Pardon".
His pronunciation already perfect
at five years old.

Sugar on Popcorn

Can I have? I will take.
It's all sugar on popcorn.
Passer à la casserole. Netflix and chill.
It's all sugar on popcorn.
I like and love. You adore and like.
I say great and let's wait. You say correct, but not right.
It's all sugar on popcorn.
I go. You leave. I do. You make.
It's all sugar on popcorn.
Across the street. Opposite the road.
The name in back, it's never before.
It's all sugar on popcorn.
I work. You bump. I talk. You parlez.
I say job. You say boulot.
I say party. You say soirée.
It's all sugar on popcorn.
In front could be next. A lot can be much.
You just arrived. I'm here. We both play touch.
It's all sugar on popcorn.

Wonderlight

There is no better view of Paris
than Jaurès on a young, hot July night.
It is fast and meaty and cut with bricks
of delightful clay and wonderlight.
Every flavor of person is here.
Bronze husbands and wives and kids.
Golden joggers. Pearl book readers.
Cream strollers. Olive friends in laughter.
And the aroma of the air
swells with gifts.
From here I can see Le Rond Point,
The train to Porte Dauphine,
A place de Clichy sign;
Two cute little brown girls with braids,
and humanity spending time in between.

Outside the Jamaican Food Spot on Nostrand, Just Off Fulton

Brooklyn's version of grand avenue:
Narrow one way with the fancy bus lane.
School kids in uniform, mothers with vibrant names.
Air B-n-B tourists dragging luggage.
Punk rock ripped jeans on Beckies and Tashas.
Lovers rock, Soul Syndicate, and Gregory Isaac.
Brooklyn's version of grand avenue.
Summer's sweet mahogany shine.
Just a walk one block east,
at the ghost of old Brooklyn crime.
Hustling street book sellers.
Winos with rare magazines.
Granny apple taxi cars.
Cops with grim faces.
The colors of blended schemes.

The Duty of a Smoker Sitting Closest to the Street at a Café in Paris

If you sit in the front row
of a café in Paris,
right where you are
closest to the street,
you know damn well
that part of this arrangement
means that you have to give
a light to every lighter-less smoker
that passes by within reach.

My Neighbors in Paris Know Me and I know Them

Today, my neighbor asked me
to buy a mouthpiece
for her boyfriend's clarinet.
Later, at the corner near métro Ternes,
just in front of sortie 1,
my other neighbor smiled
as we crossed one another in the street.
She was on her way back home,
I was on my way to the market.
Earlier, the driver at La L'Orraine
asked me how I was going.
This was after Diane paid
for the taxi ride home from Villiers.
Later, I bought a dome lamp at Habitat,
and the woman behind the counter
asked me how have I been going.

Do You Feel Free

"Said, do you feel free?"
Marine once asked me
on a slow Sunday night in Paris.
At first I thought it odd,
because no woman
in New York had ever
asked me a question
with such might.
"Yes," I said.
"I feel free.
But I've been fighting
to get here, and probably
always will be."

Because I Was Runnin' Late

When does a glance become more?
Is it in the initial capture
or is it when the moment is escaping.
Today, when I was walking
through the 8th,
on my way to the 18th,
I saw three women sitting at a café.

Each looked at me.
And damn, right, I looked at them.
Each smiled.
And you damn, right, I smiled back at them.

Each gave me some silent rap.
The first one, who looked Tunisian in flavor,
told me she would fancy riding horses with me.
The second, the one in the middle,
the one probably from Orléans,
told me it would be nice to walk with me
(as this first real taste of sunny heat
deserved such an affair.)
The third, the one on the right,
who I couldn't quite make out her background —
the one who's eyes trained on me
while I crossed the street —
told me that she had a bottle
of red wine back at her place.

I told all three of them that it all of it was possible,
but that I would have to catch them later,
because I was runnin' late.

Love, Affairs, and Broken People

Why Are They All Amazed

Women are amazed
when I tell them how deeply
I loved my ex-wife.
"So, then, why are you
not still together with her?"
Is always the same refrain.
As if love is the solution
for everything.
Love does not sign on
to rescue you when things
tilt in unexpected ways.
Love is not in charge
of cataloging all
of the layers of you
that have changed.
Love, as beautiful as it is,
is limited.
Love is something in motion,
an option to continue;
something that dares to be liquid.
Love is where you are,
where you have been,
and an negotiation
of where you want to be.
Love has its ending,
a fresh perspective,
just like everything
that begins when it's free.

I Will Jump In

I'm not the lilies type.
Flowers don't make me mushy.
But I believe in love.
I believe in that starburst of a feeling
that you get when you love somebody
and they love you back.
That citrus natural sweetness, love?
I stand up for anybody who wants that.
If you are alone and afraid
to take on love, too scared
of what it may do,
or how it might hurt you,
I promise you this:
I will jump in,
with all that I am,
and not leave you there
to fight alone.

You Would Rather

You would rather crack the shell
than smooth over this problem.
Just put the spike in,
in spite of everything
we've made and conquered.
You would rather see yourself
with the sketched face of a woman,
dull and gloomy,
save only for the flushness
of drunk vengeance.
You would rather tell me
what you don't want —
what you can no longer take,
what you won't put up with anymore —
than to speak of an item,
some morsel of what
you would still desire.
And now, in this fade
that's come to signal the end,
you would rather throw knives at me
than review your role
in our inevitable undoing.

Polite Talk at a Dinner Party

They met at a dinner party
held by a mutual friend.
They debated everything
from Aristotle to Van Peebles.
They laughed and flirted
as a side dish to the wine.
They traded stories
about old vacations
and places they'd been.
They left the party
at the same time.
They shared a taxi;
she invited him
to come inside.
In the morning,
he asked her
for her phone number.
She told him her husband
would be home around five.

For When Women Speak of Feminism on First Dates

I have never said a bad word
about a feminist.
I don't like darts to the face.
I don't care much
for the poetics of small talk
when my ignorance
is still lacking understanding.
Women are not dolls
to be tampered with.
Whatever serves their inspiration
is not for me to claim judgment.
There are some discussions,
like fits over tobacco,
that don't include me at all.
And I don't root for, or against,
any contestant on game shows
that offer prizes I can't liquidate.

Fools Like to Smell Red Roses in the Winter and Magicians Always Give Away Their Best Tricks

Nature is practical by nature,
and the same must surely go
for the downing of affairs
that stay ripe in spurts.
Everyone is smooth in the beginning:
The territories are laid bare and made clear.
Then, somebody becomes a fool,
and the quest to smell roses
in the winter freezes the track
they were racing on.
And the magicians disappear,
giving away their best trick.

Not Long After I Had Left

When you went looking
on my computer,
that time I went to Philly,
what did you expect to find?
In a maze of emails,
were you counting
on key names to guide you?
Had I said the names
of women in my sleep?
Did you think you'd know a name
from one of your many glances at my phone?
What exactly were you looking for
that you didn't already know?
Was the pull so alluring for you
that you had to smash my privacy?
That you had to spoil the good way
I'd always come to see you?
Was knowing a known so crucial
that you would forfeit the station
only you had ascended to?
Didn't I tell you that one
of the best measures of any of us
is having never taken up
certain kinds of schemes?
Did I not say to you that in seeking the proof
of someone else's harm, you harm yourself?
What was it like around 8 that morning?
Was that just the one instance?
Or had you poured through my messages
the night before, not long after I had left?

When We First Kissed

When we first kissed,
her lips tasted like
barbecue chips.
It would be years
before she would confess
that whenever
she was nervous,
she would eat
some barbecue chips.

It Was Only Supposed to Be Fun
(or, When the Walls Crumble Down on an Open Relationship Because the Whole Damn Thing Was Fraudulent from the Beginning)

It was only supposed to be fun.
The arrangement of her open relationship stipulated,
necessarily, that they could see other people.
As such, she was happy.
But not averse to having some fun
when the mood and the right man took her.
But it was only supposed to be fun.

She did not sign up for a new man to run
with her heart and turn her husband into a stranger.
She did not check the box that said,
"Fuck me whenever you please
and leave me with the receipts."
She did not ask to be delighted by a phantom
on busy weekday nights.
It was only supposed to be fun.

A few rounds of sex and some polite conversation
to make it more kosher than it really was.
Maybe a movie on a half day,
or a splurge at a candy store.
A walk on the promenade.
Some ice cream on the Lower East Side.
A quickie in some building lobby on West 78th Street.
A quickie in a fitting room
of the Victoria's Secret in King's Plaza.
A quickie in Central Park,
near where Shakespeare plays in the summer.

A quickie in Central Park,
right by the large rock overlooking
the entrance way for runners.
It was only supposed to be fun.

Crying because a man told her to keep it fun,
when it was only supposed be fun all along,
was not the predicament she volunteered for.
Becoming a text-message addict
during workday meetings,
while her boss's boss was in the room,
was not the role she thought
she would be starring in.
And skipping out on last week's
marriage counseling session,
just so her afternoon was free to have some fun,
was not the paradigm she was looking for
when she first embarked on this bright new journey.
Because it was only, just supposed to be fun.

Sex Sells

You damn right, sex sells.
Because people are doing it.
You probably did it last night.
Or this morning, or last week,
or last month. But you did it.
And even if you did or didn't do it
in any of those times,
you are probably thinking about
doing it right now.
Or when you will be doing it again,
and imagining how you'll be gettin' it in.
Because you damn right, sex sells.
Everybody is having sex,
and everybody wants to know who
is having sex, and how who is doing it.
We are not prudes — most of us anyway.
We are not neutered castaways
on a fantasy island with no working Wi-Fi.
We are not American teenagers in the 1950s,
going to our first sock hop
at the high school gymnasium
just outside of Topeka, Kansas.
We are fucking individuals
who consume sex whimsically,
thoughtfully, carelessly, cautiously,
stingily, and greedily.
Because sex sells.
And every time it sells,
we are sold on doing it again.
One more time for the road.
Just a quickie.
This time with some music on.

This time with the shades closed.
This time with the light off.
This time with the shades open.

Always More Red Wine

Ravaged by alcohol,
you ask me where's the bathroom —
in your place, a hotel room
you too know well.
Two months ago,
you were on local T.V.
receiving one of those
big fake checks,
smiling in a white summer dress.
Before that, you were the center
of a news profile, your power
and privilege displaying
in all its glory.
Now you're asking where's the bathroom
so you can go pee.
Because you want me
to hurry up and fuck you again.
Because you say I do it right.
The way you like.
Not like all the ex-others
who can keep it up
or go the length.
And you want more wine,
always more red wine.
But you can't smell the stench
of your urine on the bed beneath you.
And tomorrow, you'll send a message
asking me where did I go
and why did I leave you.
And I will remind you
that I was never there,
nor was I ever with you.

We Were a Perfect Match

I went on a date with this lady,
and I quoted a few lines from Hardy.
But she didn't know nothing at all.
I asked her about her favorite Nina Simone song,
but she couldn't seem to recall.
When the food finally came,
she reminded me that she doesn't eat meat.
Then she told me she doesn't like red wine,
only white. (I was ready to hit the street.)
When the check came, she looked at me
and waited until I grabbed it.
Which was all cool in the school
because, of course, you know I had it.
Outside the spot, we said a little small talk,
and she thanked for me the date.
Then before and I could say goodbye and turn away,
she told me her roommate wouldn't be home until late.

Lovers Will Promise Anything in Bed

Lovers will promise anything to each other in bed.
They will promise not to store your secrets
to be used later as a beating stick.
They will promise to keep you informed
about the latest misfortune that has undermined your trust.
They will promise to share the weight.
To never accuse you of spitting torpedoes
unfairly at their confessions.

Lovers will promise anything to each other in bed.
They will promise to remain faithful to the home
you had once agreed to build.
They will promise to be generous to you.
To never spoil you with the selfish candor of megalomaniacs.
And to always provide you a sanctuary of sorts.

Lovers will promise anything to each other in bed.
They will promise to be who they were when you first met.
They will promise to tell you only white lies,
or at least none that contain any significant colors.
They will promise to be kind to you.
To never be the inconsiderate voice of a sociopath.
And to always be the good listener you've never known
them for.

Lovers will promise anything to each other in bed.
They will promise that they have not seen,
heard from, or talked to their ex in years.
That any ex is just that: An *example*
of what they don't want anymore.
They will promise to never let on like they know
when you've become distant.

They will promise to never be controlling.
To never scrutinize your existence.
Or to challenge the very air that you breathe.
And they will always promise to try
to understand your ways whenever they are not busy
dealing with their own needs.

Less Than Whole

There are no tricks
to make you feel less than whole.
It has been established,
long before you ever hoped
for love or a measure of respect,
that men take.
And what men take,
more often than not,
are the bodies of women.

There are no tricks
to undress you.
It has been established,
long before you became
part of the staff,
that a drink with a man
is often but a lubricant
for his folly.

There are no tricks
to keep you quiet.
It has been established,
long before your flower
was mangled by your uncle,
and his wife, too,
that you are never to be believed.

Men do not use tricks
to capture you.
You are hunted permanently,
a loop of aggression and fury,
an indirect psychosis,

all directly aimed at taking
your body, making you
less than whole.

Advice for Men and Women in the Online Dating Age

Here's some advice for men
in the online dating age:
Do not keep her waiting,
it will only turn her to rage.
If she falls for you quick,
be certain she has fell fast before.
And be careful how close you get,
lest you turn out to be just another score.
Do not ever send her selfie pics of your dick.
But know that there will be some women
who will directly ask you to do it.
If she says she just wants to hang out and have fun,
only believe half of what she says,
because she's still hurting from the last one.
If she is 35 or older, single, with no kids,
do not play with her time,
she does not have much of it left to give.

Here's some advice for women
in the online dating age:
Do not go rushing in with every man
who visits your page.
If he tells you quickly that he is in love,
please know you are not
the only one he is thinking of.
If he says he has never met anyone like you,
know that he did last week,
and told her the same thing too.
If he doesn't tell you the names
of friends or where he likes to be,

do not trust him with secrets,
or share your dreams,
or ever give him money.

Fat & Greedy

You are just fat with no purpose.
Greedy with no reason.
Everything you want should be yours.
You ask, then you demand, then you order.
Everything is owed to you.
There's nothing you won't have.
Because you are fat with no purpose
and greedy with no reason.

You want me to be around
some of the time.
Well, that's too much.
You think it would be nice
to go somewhere for the weekend.
That's too damn long.
And this is what I mean about you:
You are just fat with no purpose
and greedy for no reason.

You want us to have dinner with your friends.
You want to go to the movies with me.
You even want to try that restaurant I like
in the 13th arrondissement.
You are unreasonable.
Because you are fat with no purpose
and greedy for no reason.

You want me to tell you stuff,
what I like and what I don't,
what I did and do, and what I won't.
You are fat with no purpose
and greedy for no damn reason.

I like making love to you,
but you want me to tell you that I do.
I think you're funny and smart and cool,
but you want to know all of that, too.
Because you are fat with no purpose
and greedy for no reason.

When we walk together I'm dazzled
by you're beauty and brand of pretty.
I stagger into places behind you
with the joy and disbelief that you are mine.
But you want to know how I feel about you.
You want some kind of symbol and sign,
because you are fat with no purpose
and greedy for no reason.

She Doesn't Want to Marry You Anymore

She didn't want to marry you anymore
because the change you promised
was more of the same.
Should she chain herself
to a never repairable you?
A man who's only pronunciation
of freedom is more women
to make love to?

Should she be confined to a lazy life
of certainly going crazy?
A bizarre timeline where you
always end up on top. Or behind.
But she never ahead?
Why would she want to look forward
to that moment when she makes
all the excuses for you? Again.
What's in it for her except
for the crumbs of your attention?

She has no expectations of you.
And to vanquish the hope of a woman
who loves so deeply is to tear apart
the tendon that fastens joy to dream.
She doesn't want to marry you anymore
because she has seen you in between.

She's seen your platform for a better job
and your plan to rebuild her faith.
She doesn't want to marry you anymore
because you have made her hate
herself more than you.

And a fate, in which you boil
this twisted recipe, surely you must know
it's one of the evils that men do.

She doesn't want to marry you anymore
because she has listened to herself
saying she no longer loves you.
She doesn't want to marry you any more
because she has wrested back her heart,
piece by piece, like an assembly worker
doing over time in the dark.

Dodge

The giddy, smashing rush of new love
is the first curse you better learn to dodge.
Celebrate the freshness of a new love,
bathe in it if you must, but do not trust
this cruel cycle, save only for your mastery
of pace and speed, want and need.

Nothing will last for as long as you think
or in the manner you surmise.
We are only equipped to adapt
to new stories with disappearing pages.
And this ain't no Merlin's magic.
The giddy, smashing rush of a new love
is the first curse you better learn to dodge.

Fall and tumble, plunge into that morning
that winks at the grand avenues facing dawn.
Splash it on your face and sniff the dew
of your thrilling new romance.
But do not get hooked on repeating this affair,
because that giddy, smashing rush of new love
is the first curse you better learn to dodge.

I have known women who are in love
with the surge at the beginning of love.
All fools looking through an artificial scope
in an old and broken time machine.
All knowing that this time, too, it will not hold.
And all looking for this loop to begin again.
I'm tellling you, that giddy, smashing rush of new love
is the first curse you better learn to dodge.

I Overheard an Ex-Girlfriend

I overheard
an ex-girlfriend
say that I was selfish.
We were alone,
siting at the kitchen table,
eating the same
Sunday breakfast.

Fuck, Make Love, and Do Shit Together

We can get fancy about it,
wax poetically or talk
heavy philosophical about it,
but we all just want somebody
we can fuck, make love to,
and do shit together with.
This has never been
a numbers thing.
No tricky algorithms,
no advice spread
in a magazine.
No speed-dating shindig
with free drinks
and a mezzanine
can displace that basic
of all basic facts
that we all just want
somebody we can fuck,
and make love to,
then kick back
and relax.

The Failure of Scorned Women and Men

Before the rebound, before that knee-jerk relationship
brought on by the recent ending of a long thing,
there is, sometimes, the scorned episode,
or what is more politely known as the revenge fuck.

In this scenario, lovers who have been displaced
from comfort zones binge on new trysts to sex away their
pain.
To avoid taking in indefinite patches of gray loneliness,
they plunge into the first people that give them a
compliment. The first people that help them to forget.
The first people that are willing to ignore their secret mess
of bludgeoned heart, fried mind, and devoured stomach.

They speak to these new suitors in tones of good times,
colors of rich lies, and shades of greedy promises.
They become pick-up artists, selfish like the thin jackets
and small purses that sit in the last empty seats
in the dives and cafés they like to meet.
They bribe themselves with a pressing confidence
of a mediocre poker player who stayed one hand too long.
And in the morning. Or late the next afternoon.
Or even two years removed from their revenge,
they speak of their failure, sometimes accidentally,
and ask if they may return again.

A Mother Teaching Her Daughter How to Ride Bikes

He will appear and disappear,
he will not stay.
He will tell you lies,
he will make you cry,
and he will leave you this way.
He will flower you with fancy words
in front of hidden notes.
He will cover you in flour
and watch you choke.
He will visit you when he wants
and give no news when he doesn't.
He will apologize with old honey,
then blame you for something.
He will borrow from you
only when he is not stealing.
He will look at you with pride
whenever you are kneeling.
He will count you as his dearest,
most trusted friend.
He will keep ongoing secrets
and betray you over and over again.
He will push inside of you
when your period swells.
He will do nothing for you
when you aren't feeling well.
He will flirt with your friends
and blame it on liquor.
He will cheat on you with your friend
and tell you he misses her.
When he is mad, you will have to be joyful.
When you are sad, he will never be helpful.

When you are dressed nicely
and feeling your best,
he will only look past you
and tell you the place is a mess.
When the game is on,
he will not entertain
any of your problems.
When he is loaded
with free time,
he still won't help you solve them.
When he drinks or stays out late
or sometimes never come home,
he will wake up in the morning
and read messages on your phone.

Soon

Soon, when the truth of your bullshit
tumbles towards you at the speed of WiFi.
When the crookedness of the doves
you've been flying find their nature.
When all of your excuses are shattered and scattered.
And when you wake up and count backwards
the days I've been gone for good.
That's when your ass is gonna realize
that everything I ever did
or said, *didn't do* or *didn't say*,
give or didn't give, get or didn't get,
was right and exact, on time, and by design.
And it will be then that all of the chirping
you've been doing to your girlfriends
will resonate as the fraud that you are.

The Good Panties

Whenever I see the good panties,
I'm like, "Let's roll!"
'Cause I know she came to play.
Won't be no half-steppin',
no foreplay instructions,
and no goofy-ass questions to fade.
When I see them good panties,
I know we gon' break a few episodes;
won't be no "I-have-to-work" sleep,
no silly shy talk,
or nothin' 'bout "let's take it slow."
When I see them good panties,
I know it's more about her than me —
There won't be no holdin' back,
no weird-ass requests,
'Cause she tryin' to get hers
off before me.

So Long As You Cherish

There is a moment when you are in love —
real love, not that soda-fiz, kiddy-bop shit —
when you're always floating on the inside,
and when every word your lady says rises
like a crescendo, or the climax in a movie
starring you in the lead as the bad motherfucker
that robs banks, and always gets away
from the cops just in time.
If you can find that kind of love,
or if it shows up at your door inexplicably
one day while you're gazing somewhere else,
hold on to it. Grip it with crazy glue.
Squeeze it with a pair of pliers.
Do whatever the fuck you have to do.
So long as you cherish that moment.

The Water Moves for the Swimmer

Begin the number with a bang.
Don't ease in.
If it looks and feels like love,
don't be the asshole inspecting seams
on cotton briefs before they ship
from the factory.
Don't occupy yourself
with trying to see
if the water's just right to jump in.
It never is.
But the water moves for the swimmer.

A Poem for Qamar

Do you remember that time
standing on the corner
of 157th Street & Broadway
and I did my first rhyme
in front of you?
But now, back up
to when we first met.
I was still a teenager
walking City College steps.
You did not like me then.
And I'm not sure why
you gave me your number
in the first place.
But I was just telling our son
that whole story again.

East Wind Writers Workshop

I Wanna Be Somebody, So Bad

"Mama, I wanna be somebody, so bad,"
she said to her mother,
stepping into a woman's red high heels.
"I know you do, Sugar —
Now, can you hand me Mama's spoon,"
her mother said.
"Mama, I know I can sing,
they ain't ready for me,"
she said, handing the spoon over.
"No, they ain't, Baby,
'cuz you got that precious voice;
Mama always told you that —
Now, can you pass me Mama's belt,"
her mother said.
"Mama, I can dance good, too.
My gym teacher said he like
the way my body moves."
"Well, now, Honey, don't you know
you get that from your mama?
We've all been some good
dancers in this family;
I know that's right —
Now can you fix me
Mama's needle
and turn down that light."

Add Water

Life is not a fact.
There is no procedure you follow
that will cook your rice the right way,
and on time.
You will have to add water.
You will have to mix the pot.
You will have to stir the whole lot
of ingredients.
There is not a search bar
or Nanny apple that can walk your bones.
Not a streaming, how-to video on YouTube.
Not an artificial device to show you the way home.
Because life is not a fact.
There is no procedure you can follow
that will give you that exact measure.
You will wake up on the same days
in a different way with a new image
of all the same people you've seen for years.
You will find yourself on a beach
of unsolvable problems.
And you will discover that you have no solutions.
Or maybe you will learn to head out for the ocean
and reshape the whole damn Q & A.
Because life is not a fact.
There is no procedure for you to follow
that will guarantee you have it made.
You will have to add water.

The Luxury of Not Thinking Anymore

You have given it no thought.
You do not have to.
Your computer shakes the potion
and serves it up as a smoothie.
You don't have to recall where you were
that time you had noodles in Vienna,
or the block you were on in Gramercy
that had those wholesale t-shirts for cheap.
Google will do it for you.
Its galaxy of bits and algorithms will tell you
exactly where you were,
and where you might want to be,
and where you will be next probably.
You don't have to think. This is the luxury.
Machines with better memories.
Machines with better peep holes
and extra value discounts on time.
Machines that vanish behind the doors
of other machines that are made up
with fuzzy lines and math from MIT,
Stanford, Silicon Valley, and Silicon Alley,
and other places where most people will never see.
This is the luxury. You don't have to think anymore.
And everything is fine. Even when the machines start
matching you with other people like you;
making predictions about your love
based on numbers that are based on sociopathic,
Uber psychotic, and humblebrag profiles.
Because we all know computers are terrifically
smart and can spot all the real lies.
Like that time they knew that the manager
at Foot Locker on Barbès was going

to shut down well before twenty.
Or that time the machine said, "J'ai envie,"
when all I meant to say was, "Je veux"
and something more simply.

How Do You Explain to a Little Black Girl Sitting in the Back Seat

How do you explain
to a little black girl
sitting in the back seat
that lots of white cops
shoot lots of black men
and America still
shows no shame.

How do you explain
to a little black girl
sitting in the back seat
that lots of white people
think lots of black people
aren't people at all,
but rather accidents
and freaks of nature
unworthy of a dime's worth
of reasonable respect
or a genuine hello.

How do you explain
to a little black girl
sitting in the back seat
that lots of black people
are target practice
to lots of white people
with guns galore
raised in violent hate,
badges of authority
authorized by the state.

How do you explain
to a little black girl
sitting in the back seat
that her mother
will not be all right,
because seeing the madness
of a killing orchestra
orchestrated right in front
of you is all wrong;
and the pillaging
of your black life
is systematic, automatic,
and endorsed by laws
made by weak men
who pretend to be strong.

Grabbing a Rocketship with One Hand and Drinking an RC Cola

I have no respect
for traditional wisdom
when it casts me aside
and tries to tell me
to sit sill in a train car
heading slow to a cliff.
I am not listening
to those instructions
about where I fit in
and who's art
I'm supposed
to be memorizing
as momentous and genius.
I am grabbing a rocketship
with one hand,
drinking an RC Cola
out the can,
and giving the middle finger
to every pernicious bastard
that can't catch my drift.

The Darkies Are on Main Street

You want me to shovel the shit, too.
But I ain't make this mess.
I'm not the one responsible for shit schools,
shitty dope, shit teachers, and shitty quotes
that only lift up those connected blacks.
Those rotten, double-crossin' motherfuckers
who speak fake prolificness,
and perfect politic tongue;
and have forgotten that we used to rap.
So, no, Jack, I'm not coming down to Main Street
to help you get all the darkies to go back home.
You have confused me, it would certainly seem,
with one of these niggers that waits obediently
for one of your leftover dog bones.

This whole thing is a farce.
Main Street ain't shit.
And you know where I'm coming from.
There was never no real Brazil uprising in America.
You didn't have to deal with no actual
Jamaican sugar cane revolt.
By all measures, Jack, you have gotten away clean.
Stealing four centuries of lives.
Snuffing out sleepless black dreams.
And takin' every damn good song we wrote.

The Great American Novel, Some Pussy on the Side, and a Few Other Things

People in America actually aim
to write the great American novel.
I don't mean all people in America.
Just the ones fed deliciously
on narrow crossroads, dubious power arcs,
or some of that shit they shovel to writers
at over-priced MFA programs.

Dig this. People in America actually set out
to write the great American novel.
I'm not talking about everybody in America,
just those dreamers who never had to use sleep
to conquer a day without eating.
I'm talking about those people rewarded
for doing basic shit, while looking basic and shit,
and the ones framing the score of the game.

People in America be trying to write
the great American novel.
This ain't everybody in America,
only the ones with shiny grammar
and fetch-me-a-dictionary prose.
The ones skiing on just-because holidays
in welcoming towns like Utah, Colorado, and Vermont.

There are people in America shooting
for the great American novel.
This ain't hard-pressed straphangers on the A train
or window washers in FiDi.
I'm talking about people like snowy hills,
sour milk, and daffodils.

People with splendid dreams that were born
of reality on their birthday.

People in America are phantom chasing,
hoping to write that great American novel.
I will assure you that this is not everybody in America.
Only those in segregated literary whirlwinds.
Those in the front applauding that grand mirage
of come you all here the same.

People in American are convinced
that they are writing the great America novel.
Not everybody in America, including me.
There are some of us who are writing
just for some pussy on the side
and a few other things.

My Mother Left a Message on My Phone

This is how I learned that my father died.
A phone telegram about a doped out man
and his wooden ending.
My mother left a message on my phone.
And she might as well told me the story
of a John Doe in a potter's grave.
Or even mention a scene from *Baretta*.
Or anything like that,
where the nameless black man
gets two in the head nonchalantly,
and a commercial for something
by Procter and Gamble comes on.

My mother left a message on my phone.
My father had died, she told me.
I listened on my way back to my car,
parked two blocks from Dawn's house.
It was on a Sunday morning,
before the churchgoers
in Canarsie were on the move.

My mother left a message on my phone.
My father had died, she told me.
I listened as I walked back to my car,
parked two blocks from Dawn's house.
And it was like that.
The news that had been in the making.
The news I never stood for because I was waiting
for that final symbol.
That one new signal to show me
the cap on a tattered and torn life
I thought I only knew for ten years.

My mother left a message on my phone.
Her voice frail and nervous, she said it twice.
The second time, you could hear
the air in the room
diving down, pulling her
somewhere behind guilt and relief.
"I just wanted to let you know
that your father died," she said.
As if there was anything "just"
about a statistical calculation
set on a man when he is born.

My mother left a message on my phone.
She wanted me to know
that my father had died.
It was a real courtesy
she was trying to extend.
And on my way driving
back home, I knew that
I was gonna have to tell Qamar
a lie about where I had been.

Your Heroes Have Holes in Their Wings

Your heroes have holes in their wings.
Ever since you've been watching them fly,
they've been walking the whole time,
fooling you on a balance beam.
Like Martin King had a thing
for blond Beckies,
Huey P liked to manage cocaine,
and Marion Barry was a crack fiend,
because your heroes have holes in their wings.

Your heroes have holes in their wings.
But you won't listen because you are too
busy kissing their ashes of amazing,
and washing their asses with jasmine
spring water soaked in rosemary casings.

You don't see that your heroes
have holes in their wings,
because you are trapped, shit deep,
in whatever better thing they've done.
You are a mosquito in the grip of a gorilla,
helpless as a spear stuck in your lung.

Idiomatic Ways of Speech
(or, Two Old Friends from East New York, Brooklyn Running in to Each Other By Chance)

"Ohhhhh, shit, look at this nigga right here!"
"Get the fuck outta here. Yo, son, I was just talkin' about your ass last night at the shop."
"Say word?!"
"Word!"
"Where the fuck you been hidin' at? I ain't seen you in adeen."
"I've been chillin' with the family. You know wifey ain't never like me in the streets."
"Yo, son, you wild hard to reach. This shortie Boog be fuckin' with was throwin' a party in the city. Free bottles for the crew. I tried to call you a couple of times to see if you wanted to come roll through."
"Son, you know I-on't answer my phone. If I ever pick up the jack, that shit is by accident.... But, yo, what's up with the family? Everybody good?"
"Everybody, good, you know. Same shit."
"You still out in Queens?"
"Same shit. But, word to my mother, son, I'm trying to move back to Brooklyn before these gentrifiers eat up all the land."

Issues in the News: A Letter to Jack

A black school teacher gets body slammed
in the street by a white cop in Austin.
She pleads for safety, for the man to, at least,
protect and serve, but he does not protect her.
Instead, he serves her with a body slam
to the ground, like they're on TV at Wrestlemania.
Except this ain't phony or for pay;
and her tears are all she has to break her fall.

Then the police chief gets on,
talkin' about, *we have Issues
of bias. Issues of racism.
Issues of people being looked at
differently because of their color.*

Jack, I call it Issues of bullshit.
Because issues are actually dealt with.
Issues are negotiated.
Issues are brought somewhere
where allegedly reasonable people
work them out by applying ways and means.

Listen, Jack, these aren't issues.
These are moments of 400 plus years
of psychosis trickling down economically
like cotton blood from pricked fingers
and leather whips from overseeing hands.
These are moments that police chiefs
in Texas still don't understand.

Get Down to It

People who don't have shit to say
are always the ones spending
the most time dressing up
their language with extra
over coats and pullovers.
Get to the MOTHERFUCKIN' point.
Tell it like it is.
Push the words
in a wheel barrel
if you have to.
Or drop them
as broken fiber glass.
But get down to it.
Say it how you really feel.
Because that's the only way
your meaning is gonna last with me.

Pay Me

I'm not giving any
of you motherfuckers
a piece of my mind for free.
This world spins for me
in certain circumstances
and with backdrops
of well-understood colors.
I don't do mediocre shit,
with mediocre language,
and a mediocre understanding
of what rhythm is.
I don't expect for my story
to be celebrated or pinned
in praise or selected
as a prime line by a narrow honcho
riffling off this year's sure shot.
Fuck that. Pay me.
I'm not giving any
of you motherfuckers
a piece of my mind for free.
This world spins for me
in a way some you ain't never seen.
A collision of blues and streams
of views I have fused together
and welded at the seam.
I am not a common collaborator.
I am not always on the grid.
And I am not at a dearth
for friends or places to be.
I don't skate on mountain tops
selling hope. I deal in the what is.
I arrange it so as to make things bright.

I have fought. I have been in fights.
I have tasted my own blood
from the violent cuts of life.
So I ain't giving any of you motherfuckers
a piece of my mind for free.
You will pay me.
And we will call it a fair trade.
And I won't bring up the fact
You still owe me change.

You Better Read

One thing you better do
with your life is read.
Don't talk to me about anything else,
unless you've read something first.
People on the outside of books,
and magazines, and liner notes,
and essays, and poems,
and street signs, and short stories,
and sub-titles just can't be trusted.
Who in their good mind would turn
away from eating up knowledge?
Turn away from scoring the only diet
that lets you get fat and lean
and laid in between?
Turn away from spoonfills
of different universes of light?
What reasonable type would trash
the chance at gaining something?
Gaining a new mission?
Gaining a brand new stream?
Gaining a fresh premonition?
Gaining some more steam?

The Bleachers
(And We Shall Speak Again, Tomorrow)

Up here in the bleachers,
sitting with Satchel,
watching *Bingo Long's Traveling All-Stars
and Motor Kings*.
Listening to Coltrane's solo on *So What*.
We catch word that the slang
has changed again, and the new Negro
is now post-black. Cans of my father's
Schlitz Malt Liquor pass around,
and we talk shit as we kick back.
We laugh at the pomp of these new niggas
who still feel secure. Satch speaks again
of how the Majors blew it.
And of when his love
for the game was pure.
We disagree over who's finer,
Diahann Carroll or Dinah Washington.
Nancy Wilson, or Claudine. Cleopatra Jones,
Phyllis Hyman, or the only Josephine.
Then we agree on the math that made Obama.
The slash carved across scarred faces.
And Plato's republican drama.
The downfall of Sparta.
And the fallen Kings of man throughout the ages.

Is It Because I'm Black
(Dedicated to Uncle Syl Johnson)

Is it because I'm black,
the only time you see me
is when it's time to shoot.
Or harass. Or leave back.
Or look at me like that?
Like I'm a people snuffer;
one dog of a lover;
a terrific dancer;
an old lady mugger?

Is it because I'm black,
you won't let me in,
or pay my old bill,
that you charged?

Is it because I'm black,
that you don't expect nothin' from me?
That I have no decency, no ideology,
no reason or cause,
no Kant or Hume in my faculty;
not even my own damn memory?

Is it because I'm black,
that I excel, despite all of your shit.
Despite all the bull you kick.
Despite all the times like this?

Is it because I'm black,
we both know I'm one
bad motherfucker?

An ocean coaster.
A purple Crown Royal bag
full of priceless oysters?

Is it because I'm black,
you take everything I invent,
and do it all wrong,
then get mad because I already
created some new shit?

Is it because I'm black,
that you mad that you
can't fuck like me.
Mad that you can't be this free.
Mad that you can't talk so greasy.
Mad that you can't ever be me?

Black People Jump High

We've been leaping
all our lives.
It's a wonder
why you don't look up
and see people
skipping across
building tops everyday.

Leaping to get somewhere.
Leaping to get something.
Leaping to be somebody.
Leaping to get away.

We've been leaping
all our lives,
it's a wonder
why you don't look up
and see people
falling down
from building tops everyday.

Generation Nothing

You thought the "x" stood for "exciting",
"any possibility", "the absolute",
"the absolute unknown",
"the absolute anything",
"the ultimate", "cross culture",
"cross color", "crossing point",
or some shit like that?
Wrong.
If you were born in America,
between 1965 and 1980,
your parents, and your parents' parents,
labeled you nothing.
Generation X. Generation Nothing.
Supreme slackers.
The one's with no scope.
The minimalizers with no hope.
The incomplete, ungrateful, lost and twisted;
the thoughtless, the worthless,
the ones bound by every limit.
Generation nothing.
You had no chance.
You were the left over frozen food
of the baby boomers.
The piss water of the generation
that killed Adolf Hitler.
You were the nothing generation on arrival.
Expected to do nothing,
be nothing, or count for nothing.

A Rhyme for Qamar
(That's Why Amir is So Wild)

It always starts with the Roof Top/..
'Cuz back when I was thinkin' of sure shots/..
Hopin' I would never get shot/
Playin' the block/
You hated me when-we-met/...
'Member chicken at Wells?/
That time up in Harlem when it didn't go well?
I didn't like you/ You was stuck up/
Still smash, though/
I was smoking 'hash in your lobby,
and let them know niggas who I was/
'Cuz you know, I-know-the-street/..and that's love/.
Remember when Gary and Carl got shot with them slugs?
On New Years? You kept me in the house for a minute/..
We kissed on the clock/ .I broke out n' bought a Guinness/..
That could've of been me/
'Cuz I was thirty minutes from the crime/....
the same amount of time ..you kept me chillin' inside/...
And I knew/ You would be the mother to my child/...
A fighter like me/... That's why Amir is so wild.

The Classics

A Poem for Spring

We call on Spring with green hope
shined across our face.
Her voice a honey whistle.
Her arms a warm felt,
brushing against our weight.

How she leads us through
Summer's door, optimism in ripe peach.
Her sweetest fruits blossom.
Her lightest sounds heard,
gazing upon our speech.

All the Fools Rush in the Rain

All the fools rush
in the rain.
This splendor
of nature's silk green
forever stain.
Holding back
the sure light
of the sun.
You see them
take speed,
no flight yet run.

You Love Not Me

You love not me.
And this slowing time warned you.
Yet you still don't see.
Yes, the idea of something you wished before.
The hunger for which sweetens the meal.
Fed by a torn wedding brochure.
And so the last began with the first pill.
Staggered I, when I saw your mouth
hung open in a bathtub sea.
Blood from your wrist flowing south.
I am sure, you love not me.

A Poem for Jamie Claar

How much fantastic is leftover
on the streets of New York?
On 67th Street & Broadway,
we had our own fare,
a festival of enlightenment,
a celebration in the late August rush
of corner symposiums and casual fun.
To go back there again, only to see
how grand things would become.
To trust someone is human.
To trust a New Yorker is a chance.
But when such bonds emerge,
the force is as strong as marble,
as solid as landmark stone.

All That Melts

As the plan escapes the thought,
so goes the achievement.
Washed away with every season.
As man shapes the field
and plant steel at dusk,
beliefs held tightly
soon flake from rust.
As infants soar boldly
through blades of grass,
their shadows age
from yesterday,
their voices lay flat.
As kings ache
from powers torn
and fear left stripped,
all that melts reforms;
all that is solid shifts.

Ask Me Where I've Been

You can ask me where I've been.
I won't always tell you.
I won't always tell you
what crack being cut
on a porcelain plate sounds like;
or where I was when heard that sound.

You can ask me where I've been.
But I probably won't always tell you
about the perceptions well guarded
at a New York literary party;
or where the crystal of privilege
likes to rest its anchor.

You can ask me where I've been.
And I might tell you why
some Thai food in Les Batignolles
overtook Mexican food
as my favorite cuisine.

Ask me where I've been,
and I'm more likely to point you
somewhere over canyons
than I am to bring you close
to the top of a rain drop.

A Poem for My Brooklyn Crew

We have made it through.
Caught up to being
real-time adults
with plain problems.
A bunch of squares
with memories
and permanent scars.
Rough cuts
from dangerous stars.
My Brooklyn Crew
who's solemn.
Steve (Stax).
Mike (Rone).
Brian (Boog).
E (Eion).
And me (Sa).
making five.
My debt to all
of you is more
than a promissory note.
My love for you,
my noble Brooklyn crew,
always stays alive.

So Clear of Victory

What force of poisoned dart
summons a man to self destruct,
so clearly past victory.
What notion of beggar's luck
or empty brush
soon paints him his own misery.
What pillar surely won overwhelms
his course to savage surrender,
so clear of victory.
What does he not remember
in that flash in December
that shot gun hole needs no memory.
What grand buffet sours a man
to eat no more,
so well past victory.
Which shadow or deadly medal
prompts him to war
that feeds his self enmity.

What Will They Know?
(Poem #2 for my Son, Amir)

What will they know
about a living room
turned into a basketball court?
Gaffing tape, precise black marks
where I first taught
you your shot.

What will they know
about your smiling
sprint towards Fajr?
In the couplets
of small talk,
at the parties
I usually avoid,
what will they know
about you having
never heard your
grandfather's voice?

What will they know
about the grace
at *Les 4 Saisons*,
or the familiar faces
at Ménilmontant?
When women from Holland
speak of women from Africa
who wear wigs and weaves,
what will they know
about the weight
of Western history.

What will they know
about you having
never heard your
grandfather's advice,
first hand?
Near Oberkampf,
along the brief stretch
that ebbs and seems
like a small north Brooklyn,
what will they know
about Truffaut,
or how we beat the system?

What will they know
of Hitchcock, Ajax or Eddie,
Van Peebles, Portier, or Freddie?
Gordon Parks and the Gordon Parks
that followed him?
Of our late walks
through dix-septième.
Where we leaned as we do
into our canvas of design.
What will they know
about the rumbling
patience this city
moves to foster,
or the rules we've made
for sketching each line?

Certainty is the Fool's Tambourine

Against the proud brow of luck
and the option of taking a chance,
is there always only a few of us
with concrete in our gut
and conviction in our dreams?
Certainty is the fool's tambourine
playing loudly in a crowded room
filled with bad acoustics and mildew,
and running water streaming towards
all the power sockets in the walls.
This is why scientists and pushers
both know the score of laws.
The math is arranged in the same etiquette.
The compulsive brain is always building rocketships
that blast wherever the wind goes.
Why don't more people believe
in what's residing out there?
Why don't more people oil their wrists
and ankles, and slip out of the shackles
that steal their journeys and confiscate
their belief in the fascinating?

The Fair Lady of Baskerville

Do not assume that you will understand
what measures man will take and make women till.
What by design was her only hope.
Or rather it be to hang the rope.
This is what spoke to the fair lady of Baskerville.

Days that set in with bruise,
outmatched by cruel nights a tortuous drill.
Dissolving into her typeface work.
Until this too suffered hurt.
What unusual courage fair lady of Baskerville.
Does not cigarette burns on the spine,
or belt whipping cause to kill?
Thunderous punches to the eye.
Savage kicks on floors to break thigh?

So seem fitting why the stabbing
becomes this woman's will.
Do not assume that the docile
will not have a taste that blood spill.
Neither small frame or strength.
Love of Spring rain and its scent.
Such is murder by the fair lady of Baskerville.

A Poem for Sheila Frazier

Georgia.
I will always know you as Georgia,
so pardon the crush of a young black boy
that has never gone away.
You were Priest's real lady,
not that monotone ofay
who only wanted him
for his coke and jungle brag.
Imagine if I'd never seen
that bathtub scene?
Imagine what I would think
about love in movies,
or what my future would mean.
Or how I felt about myself
every time I didn't see me
on the big screen?

Simple Equations

The Lethality
of the equation:
Money and greed.
The challenge
of circumstance:
A poor mouth to feed.
The rude mix
of machines and guns:
The weaponry of the rich
engulfed in fun.
The hollowed advance
of an illiterate teen:
The melting dynasty
of a wayward king.

A Poem for Marina Keegan

The completion of a path is not a given thing.
A little girl laughing in the playground,
the songs of morning birds in the spring.
The promise of new space and fresh land.
A challenge of aging in the Big City.
The solace found glowing in a writer's hand.
The course of nature performing its show.
A woman on the verge of casting her beam.
The completion of a path is not a given thing.

The Future of Goodbye

There is never a goodbye,
but only the feeling
of the treasure that endures.
Along the grand avenues
or the small cobbled roads,
there are memories to guide you.
Like the profound art
of yesterday's mention,
you are a blaze of mercury, a vision
of speed that remains
as much as it goes.
In this reminder,
this trail that requires
a certain blend
of light and dark,
you are embraced,
steadied by the notion
that more things return
than they leave.

Knowledge is a Reward Most Giving

Knowledge is a reward most giving.
To know of something is to be living.
To grasp the mechanics of an engine's scope.
To recite the milk of an ancient quote.
Knowledge is a reward most giving.

Knowledge is a reward most giving.
To hear a sound and know its meaning.
To gaze at a star and feel it's shine.
To fade from the bar when you know it's time.
Knowledge is a reward most giving.

A Poem for Clara

My blunder of magnificent arrogance
blacked out what you had on offer.
Gentile, with a punchy directness
and a celebrating smile,
a soft bounce in your voice,
and a mix of joy and the flakes
of sunset in summer waltzing
in your face. And I, the villain of man,
pressing his successes and accomplishments,
turning your invitation slowly against me.
Yet you stayed and listened to me pitch.
You put a friend on hold,
someone who had properly earned
your trust already.
And for what? Me?
A lasting look or a glance
at the shape made from our beginning.
In boasts shielded in sarcasm,
I made bold promises of a night
with no requisite enchantment.
And you still smiled;
never broke from the posture
that beautiful hearts like yours
always keep steady.
You laughed even.
And I thought about that time
somewhere in the future,
after the decorated promises,
believing that we were already
together, making fun
of this time when you knew
more and I knew less.

My First Touch of Spring

When I was young and the girls
passed the boys notes,
after when movies and television
was the only thing left
to remind me of where I go
on sleepless nights
from me doing guard duty,
I had my first touch of Spring.

When we would still remember
phone numbers by heart,
when I had a crush on every one
of my older cousin's girlfriends
in dresses, jumpers, tennis skirts,
shorts, leather jackets, and jeans,
I had my first touch of Spring.

When I used to see Marisol
in the hallway,
before Makeeba gave my bag full
of Jolly Ranchers away,
before I kissed Kimberly
under the tortious shell,
and before Booby died
from gun shot sprays,
I had my first touch of Spring.

When Marisol used to call me
on the phone,
before I'd ripped up two
of her notes in disbelief,
before I used my Smith Corona for sleep,

and before we kissed
each other on the lips,
I had my first touch of Spring.

When Marisol used to laugh
and hug me,
after she used to cry
and share with me,
after she told me of all
the things she would be,
after we had our first
and only fight,
and before she never
woke up that last midnight,
I had my first touch of Spring.

Artificial Intelligence (A.I.)

We have always shaped stone
and created sage.
Mastered the agony
of changing time.
Balanced our hopes
on the coming age.
Bargained away our humanity
to advance the line.

With vigor of giants
with greedy hands,
We orchestrated the future
with raging trust.
Ripping through centuries
and bleaching lands.
We have always made the machines
that will see us crushed.

A Poem for Uncle Prince

Here's what happened.
You were a renegade.
An actual music revolution,
no pun intended,
but the meaning stays the same.
Your sky rocket soared
before the network age.
At a time when rhyme was rhyme
and when MTV let videos play.
Your journey was Stevie Wonder songs
in the key of life, Sly Stone and motor funk,
Village Voice write-ups,
purple hogs, and villain's punk.
You were shackled to the future.
And when it came back around again,
you were on the other side of the chain;
your go-crazy days now an intruder
outside the voiture that has no train.
They called you a genius, a visionary,
a vanguard ahead of time,
a pistol six-shooter in a saloon,
but then came auto tune,
and you were quickly cast aside.

Looking At Picture Books With a 3-Year-Old Boy Who Already Reads and Watches Alfred Hitchock Movies at Lunch
(Poem #3 for My Son, Amir)

My son had an Imagine Kit
(ask him about it),
or an I-Kit, we sometimes
called it for short.
That's all he ever knew
what a bookshelf was.
Until he needed a new Imagine Kit,
and he saw me looking
online at bookshelves.
"Oh, man, that's a whole lot
of I-Kits, Pop," he said to me.
"And so then, what's a bookshelf?"
he asked me…
Amir was an early reader,
one who ravished everything
that had a spine and words on the page.
So looking at picture books with him
was a privilege and a gesture of art.
He glued his own words to every image.

Hills of Grass

When we've all handed the rest
of ourselves to the networks
and the machines,
then we go out
for picnics in the park,
or walks by rivers,
or parties at clubs
lined with robot bouncers,
we will read — on monuments
erected by the machines
all around us —
"Leave them something."
Yet, somewhere else inside
of the latest computer designed
version of grammar school,
a little boy will be drawing wavy trees
and a little girl will be sketching hills of grass.

A Writer I Knew Gave Herself a Man's Name

A writer I knew gave herself
a man's name.
Jumping behind the wheel
of a truck, as such.
She thought she was buying fame.
Scratching at opportunity,
lunging her identity
into a grave she saved.
"Only if it was necessary," she said,
She would do it, if she had to pay.

Let Me Tell You About My Son, Amir (Poem #4 for My Son, Amir)

Go find me the most
courageous man that you know.
Then point me in the direction
of the man that he looks up to,
and what you will then see
is that man looking, curiously,
at Amir sitting on the side
of a mountain —
that's restricted to all else —
eating Haribo Gold Bears,
and writing notes
on canvas paper
about the new ways
Allah may allow him
to touch this world.

Garbage Lady

Bending over on swollen old legs,
into a green wastebasket,
scavaging for a day's worth to eat.
For what crime did this punishment
visit this lady who digs through our garbage;
who thrives on our throwaways from the week?
Pushing a wobbly cart up a hilled road,
into no set place to be;
gasping for a drink of life.
For what indiscretion did this curse
fall upon this lady who bears like atlas.
Who drags her body through the blades of night.

The Arrogant Masters of Time

Man is at his most arrogant
when he is considering time.
He thinks himself a master of it,
so he needs not bother with its design.
When he is young,
before he has matched words to meaning,
before he has stood on his own,
he does not have a sense for time.
When he is somewhat older,
in the canyon of his first loves seeming,
he believes himself to control its prism in his mind.
Crashing into experiences,
spending the currencies of his next days.
Aged firmly and too far gone,
he sees the cost of what he pays.

Love of Forsaken Town

Oh, love of forsaken town,
please send back your thunderous punch.
Surely you know the cruelness in this sport.
To see her again, nay, to just to hear her voice
once more speak to my frozen joy
would be the calm on snowy pond.

Oh, love of forsaken town,
consider true your reversal.
For isn't an exception a mandatory waiver
in a case such as mine?
Have you not seen her?
The almond complexion,
the delicately placed dimples,
the curve of her hips,
the exactness of her design?

Oh, love of forsaken town,
give this woman back to me.
I was mad to have loaned you her.
It is my right to take what still belongs me.

Oh, love of forsaken town,
I warn you that I will fill you whole.
That I shall make your belly gluttonous
with discarded women.
If you do not give her back to me,
I will make you a population
of suffering damsels.
By noon today is all you have.
If she is not returned to me by then,
I shall have began.

If Today Was When We Met

Gorgeous legacy of pearl beauty and curious mind,
if today was when we met, we would not be so unkind.
We would not be a league of two spies.
Hiding secrets in places neither have seen.
Spitting nectar from serpents;
building factories of lies.
Murdering the other in our dreams.
Looking at you now,
I would surrender anything to forget.
Oh, how we would be in love again
if today was when we met.

The Rangers

The Rangers came upon a Mexican farmer
walking in the desert and they asked,
"Have you seen Time
and the clock that rides with him."
The Mexican, looked up, shielding his hands
from the sun, and said,
"You are eight on horses, searching for Time,
whom you seem to know well.
And I am one quite acquainted with the clock;
for I have only seeds to grow.
But alas, my duty is to help
guide lost men like you at large,
so I will make fast my charge.
Time is resting back where you came from.
At the place your massacre went.
And the clock which you say rides along with time
does but carry my name;
which is the same as your old conscience."

A False Invention

Who speaks of grounded dreams.
Of limits where no man dare beams.
The aspirations all put to rest.
The chance to grab piece of Sky.
What then gathered makes happiness?
Who tells what be for you or I?

What grand dictator seeks to mention
is not but only a false invention.
Are we not slaves to the same rule?
We all shall be spelled by death.
Why then honor a fool?
Such grievance does earn my protest.

Crest and Crown

So man is born with free will in his fate.
Then each is guardian of his own estate.
And so, is not hubris among the easiest ills?
This worth of ours valued above all else.
No treaty kept, except one's own meals.
The profit in considering only himself.
Then each is king of his own court.
No better faculty found.
In all circumstance, he is living,
nay, dying to protect his crest and crown.

The Spoils of Humanity

The Dimming Glow of Youth
(or, Posing Not Far From République)

What will any of you dare to be
in this age of connection and instant show?
Will the snap of desire fall recklessly
too soon before you put in the work
for which all things of real worth demand?
Maybe you have only seen a dream as a phrase,
no more than the rail of a laugh
or the stillness of a selfie engaged.
Posing not far from République,
what will any of you fail to detect
about the promise of stars
and the dimming glow of youth.
Mightiest among you are both
the quiet and rambunctious,
the timid and the boisterous.
For you, does the talk of wars
and the assemblage of history
govern any requisite idea?
Are you any less bound to fate
than the woman scratching for food
in the bottom of a garbage can?

Why Would Anyone Care About Me

I've done nothing famous,
been nowhere exotic, she said,
weighing the gravity
of telling the story
of a little girl stolen
by her mother's demons.

The First Place We'll Eat Together

To be done with life at 35 is odd.
Calling quits on a journey seven years in
don't seem reasonable in an age of new ways
and extra-size localization.

When you told me on the plane to Paris,
I did not offer you a hidden look of understanding.
If we had known each other better,
I would have vaporized your decision
for the cowardice that it was.

New York beats up everybody.
Same if you paint. Same if you dance.
But this, above all, is what has left you scuttled.
It's not that you have sold your imagination
or bartered your talent.
It's that you have laid down to the Apple's crunch.

When you first came to NYC,
the world was in front of you,
a tapestry simply yours for discovering.
And you ran this way for a while,
living off nothing but the fuel
of a New York City dream.

But then, the truth about New York
surrounded you. And you surrendered.
The shame in that is not that you folded up
or that you made queries as to the why of your endeavor.
To be burned out is a fantastic commonplace
in my dear deranged New York.

The tragedy is that you betrayed your value
and cut loose because the mechanics
of the art system wouldn't let you in.
So now you come back to Paris.
And you're all aglow with the thought
of the first place we'll eat together.

Too Far Gone

In her twenties, she was a student,
a burlesque dancer downtown,
a photographer, a waitress,
the lead singer of a band,
a phone sex operator
with a beautiful sound.
She ate quickly.
And quoted Nikki Giovanni,
Angela Davis, Professor Stein,
Nora Ephron, songs by The Smiths,
Paul Simon, and James Brown lines.

In her thirties, she picked the coke back up,
then breezed and let it drop for good.
She moved four times around Brooklyn,
then chose an old Manhattan hood.
At dinner parties, she was the delight.
The funny one in the room.
The one with the brightest mind.
The one who made other ladies swoon.
When you asked her, "Where's your boyfriend?"
She'd reply, "I'm not defined by him."
If you asked her, "When are you getting married?"
She'd answer, "Is it always about him?"

In her forties, she went back to school
and grabbed a second graduate degree.
She moved back to Brooklyn, this time
in Bed Stuy, near where I used to be.
She took up online dating,
binging at least twice a week.
She started smoking weed again,

drinking more, and doing extra sleep.
She ate her food with a slower demeanor.
She thought about the children she didn't have
and how her clock was on the fever.

In her fifties, she took a weekend gig
and brought in a roommate.
She started writing personal essays,
mostly about a life stopped short too late.
She went on dates whenever she could.
She told lies about her age
and hoped they understood.
And in the morning,
after midnight was on,
she cried herself to sleep,
knowing she was too far gone.

She Could Not Wait (for K.E.)

She knew they were coming
for this year's Christmas dinner.
He and her father had been
Friends for more than thirty years.
And His Wife knew
her mother for nearly the same.
They were family.

When her parents traveled
for business, that's where she stayed.
She even had her own room
at there place, a play room.
They called it.

It was filled with toys.
And there was a gumball machine.
And a special loveseat where
He used to tell her stories
while his Wife watched.

And in her play room,
as He and His Wife called it,
there was a polaroid camera
and a king size bed
for them all to sleep.

Whenever she was scared —
because 8 year olds
are frightened by Monsters —
they would insist
that she would be safer
if they all slept together.

So in this room,
Their play room,
she would lie in bed,
numb from head to toe,
neither scared nor alive
to how He and His Wife
were keeping her safe.

When she turned 13,
her father was promoted.
And with his new promotion,
he no longer had to travel;
and she no longer had to go
to the Play Room.

Now, 19, and back home
from college for Christmas break,
her father told her that They
were on Their way
and would be there soon.
And all she said was
she could not wait.

Rumi Says Pay Attention to How Things Blend and Eddie Says He Knows It's a Rotten Game

I've read poems about love,
life, and death.
And I've seen movies
about the death in living,
and love without a sure life to feed.
Rumi cautions about paying attention
to how things blend, and cutting down
the focus on good and bad.
Sounds like privilege to me.
Because I'm with Eddie:
It is a rotten game.
And the only blending that I see
taking place is that kind of blending
that's permitting me and the other Eddie's
nothing but a non-blending.
Non-equality.
Non-equity.
Non-me, especially.

A Bird Looking Back At You Curiously

A bird staring back at you
means you have caught flight.
You have plunged without
any wings or means to steady,
or even to reverse your fall.
On second thought,
does you no good right now.
Whatever treaty you couldn't reach,
back before you stepped off this ledge,
has already been recorded.
A stat you won't ever see.
Because a bird looking back at you curiously
means you have come undone;
pounded into somebody's memory.

Most Girls Grow Up to Be Brave Women

The first time I rode a horse,
a little girl asked me,
"What's your horse's name?"
I said I don't know.
And she said,
"Well, how can you ride a horse
if you don't know it's name?"
This is when I knew
that most girls grow up
to be brave women.

Be Leery of Their Disguise

Be leery of those
who try to disguise themselves
by changing hate terminology
into popular language.
Watch the gates for the commanders
who try to disguise themselves
as saviors of your freedom
by telling you to turn in
the wildness of your mind
for the placid dusk jacket
that binds a dictator's manifesto.

When We Switched on Computers

We used to switch computers on
in the morning, usually for work,
then cut them off promptly
when the day was done.
But now, the day is never done.
And the weeks don't take curtain calls.
And the month's never grab sleep.
And the years never cease.
Because we are always on now.
And our computers have tricked us
into believing that they call all the shots.
We no longer switch on computers
unless we need to kick start them again.
In which case, they are not really cut off,
they are only paused, placed in reboot mode,
while we go to our other computer
that is just as connected, just as demanding,
just as enabling, and always stuck
in a perpetual state of always.
When we used turn computers on,
there were two handfuls of T.V. shows
and one handful of channels.
When we used to turn computers on,
we knew only what our friends told us,
not what their Facebook statuses
implied, revealed, or lied about.
When we switched computers on,
we stayed away from the screens
because of the headaches
they were sure to dish out.
Now, when we're not looking
at a computer screen, we are detached.

And the detachment gives way to headaches.
And the headaches give way to pain.
And the pain rushes to eclipse us
if we go too long without checking the screen.
Any screen. Smart phone. Laptop. Desktop.
Even the names are a mirage against us
really seeing what happened
when we switched computers on.

Samuel Jackson Don't Say No to Movies

If you wait for when it's perfect, for when it's optimal
to pull off the things you dream up,
you have already punctured your beacon and call,
because Samuel Jackson don't say no to movies.
If you are begging for somebody to squeeze the clock,
or if you are saving that new road for taking
when everything is just right,
you have already scorned your chance,
because Samuel Jackson don't say no to movies.
If you are invited to blend your wonder and savvy
with a maybe next-big-thing,
and you waver and don't go,
you have already resigned your spot
on the bus to Famesville,
because Samuel Jackson don't say no to movies.
There are no perfect moments.
There are only moments.
We splash them with the tools of our distinction,
or we watch them vanish in the air.
Because Samuel Jackson don't say no to movies.
Because Samuel Jackson don't say no to movies.
Because, Samuel Jackson, don't say no to movies.

The More You Know, the More You Will Lose People

Learn something new and call it a good thing.
A refreshing reward, an artifact of the pursuit
of knowledge or the quenching of curiosity.
But dig this: The more you know,
the more you will lose people.
Decipher the odds behind black jack.
Stroll alongside the Grand Canyon,
learn the stride of Phoenix and Flagstaff.
But unless they are with you,
unless they have been there,
unless they have something fair to trade,
they will not be around for long,
because the more you know,
the more you will lose people.
Dig into the throws of Sartre and Kant,
J.J. Walker, Du Bois, or Duchamp.
Highlight that line from that Shakespeare play
where the uncle does in his brother.
Press rewind on Hathaway's little ghetto boy.
Trace the fall of the Ming Dynasty.
Call up lines from Anne Frank's diary.
But if those close to you can't dig or highlight,
rewind, trace, or call it right along with you,
they will be gone soon,
because the more your know,
the more you will lose people.

You Will Know Somebody

You will know somebody
that voted for Donald Trump,
because people lie about their beliefs.
You will know somebody
that swims silently in a bottle,
because people hide their grief.

You will know somebody
that cuts a sharp tongue,
that never seems to have any fun,
or laugh at the joker when he makes
light of the world.
Because people shield the cleaner,
un-detoxed versions of who they are,
and never include you in their twirl.

You will know somebody
that is a stranger to charity.
You will know somebody
that gives without cause,
reason, or residue.
Because people move along fault lies
you are not entitled to.

You will know somebody
that splurges for sex.
You will know somebody
that claws back every compliment.
Because people spend workable hours
coming up with new ways to throw
you off their scent.

You will know somebody
that gets away to new places
with luggage engulfed
by hidden secrets.
You will know somebody
that talks too much.
You will know somebody
that guards every word
in every sequence.

You will know somebody
that will never bother to tell
you what is really going on,
or what they did,
or where they were,
or who they were with
that time last week.
Because people presume
to be fluid and prefer not to be
found out until the coast is clear;
long after they've got you beat.

If You Allow Yourself to Be Invisible

You are invisible,
so long as you let them
count you as the other.
You do not count,
so long as you let them
sweep you to the side
like a broken wafer.
You don't amount to shit,
so long as you allow them
to snap your ideas and thoughts
into shards of plastic cartoons
and one-liner jokes about the monkey,
the bitch, the nigger,
or the witch in the room.
You are the other,
so long as you let them cast you
as some dynasty of freakism,
still plagued by your inability
to suffer the bullshit or swallow
the island Kool Aid.
You don't register,
so long as you allow them
to steal your application to live;
to do all the things in life worth doing.
Like singing in your own voice
and re-thinking again
after you've made your choice.
You will not be seated,
so long as you allow them
to tell you how to stand,
and which mirror to look into,
and what notions to claim.

If you allow them to instruct you
on the details of your order,
the minutia of which borders
you fear, or the horizons you hold dear,
then you will be invisible.

Go Deeper

It ain't easy being me/... I spit college degrees/... I hit the mic until it's beat up/... I'm as wild as they be/... I'm a stamp, flying to places/... A razor, on a face lift/... A champ driver, with greatness/...The reason for a racist to fear/... Up on the Brooklyn Bridge, drunk from some beer/... Up in the old, Albee Square/.. buyin', fashionable gear/... Up on Jaurès, drinking wine/... I see my rhymin' more clear/... Up in Barbès Rochechouart/.. they know my name, I've been there/... Fix some food from the market/... I'm simple/.. I read knowledge/... I'm bruised up from livin'/.. I'm peaceful/..follow the Prophet/... My jewels fall on the carpet/... I vacuum with clean commas/... My rappin' is a scheme/.... My meters cary a sonnet/.... I coast, while people stuck, walkin', backwards in time/... I quote, from my own diary/..the truth in my lines/... The proof, is in the size/.. I'm at large/.An editor/.. note, takin'/... competitor/... chasin' .. a real story/.... . A Pepsi, ..broke over, burger/... I got friends who was murdered/... Plus, family and some colleagues/... That's part of my nurture/.... 'Dre took took the bait/.. And caught a shottie instead/... Booby, was always dumb/... His homicide, could be read/... White girls from L.E.S. try to get in my head/... I keep my distance/...My premonition is to fuck 'em, and jet/... Put me next to a scholar/... .We ain't, the same, people/... A make books that's popular/... My words/.. Go/.. Deeper

Acknowledgements

Amir Ali Said, my son, best friend, and Superchamp cofounder— Thank you for your love, friendship, knowledge, courage, and curiosity, and also for your always smart, enthusiastic, and timely editorial advice (and copyediting). Remember, all the answers are in three places: Q, S, and YT. Samir Arts next.   Qamar, my son's mother, my ex-wife — Your love, belief, and support through the years has meant (and will always mean) something special to me. Thank you.

G. Ferguson, my editor — Thank you, Ferguson. You continue to stay on point. My East New York crew — Eion, Stax, Rone, and B, I owe a tremendous debt to you all. Although we don't see each other (as much, or at all) like we did years ago, NYC would have never been my NYC without you. "Fuck that, give all my peoples a seat up front." Salute! Mariella Gross, thank you for your unwavering commitment, your refreshing worldview, and your willingness to challenge yourself. And for an extra round of copyediting whenever needed. Jamie Claar, thank you for always having a good word and honest feedback. And thank you dearly for you kindness and support. Looking foward to your stewardhip of Superchamp Books acquisitions. Veronique, thank you for *À Table*! and more. Samir, thank you for showing me around and inviting me everywhere. You are friend. Théo, thank you for your kindness and your interest in my work. I look forward to working with you on future projects here in France. Tiphaine, your patience is incredible. It's only outmatched by your directness or your sense for humanity. Thank you. Rahel, thank you for being real. Lorenzo, I have more than one project in mind that can use your wit and sharpness. Sami, thank you for always looking after me at Le Jaurès, *même chose semaine prochaine.* Marine, thank you for caring deeply and for teaching me so much. Barry Wallenstein, you knew and you encouraged me. Thank you.

About The Author

Amir Said is a writer, publisher, musician, and father from Brooklyn, NY. In addition to writing and managing the BeatTips Network of music education websites, Said also runs Superchamp Books, an independent publishing company. He is the founder of BeatTips, the leading resource for beatmaking/hip hop production education; and he has written a number of books, including *The Truth About New York*, *The BeatTips Manual*, *The Art of Sampling*, *Ghetto Brother*, and *The Truth About Paris* (co-written with John McNulty). His new novels, *Going Down to the Bungalow Bar* and *Feed the Meter*, are forthcoming in 2017 respectively. His album *The Best of Times* was released in the fall of 2016.

www.ingramcontent.com/pod-product-compliance
Lightning Source LLC
Chambersburg PA
CBHW050122020526
44112CB00035B/2358